KAPPIYA'S PICTURE BOOK - 2

BIRDS ALPHABET

KAPPIYA CLASSICS

Contents

FOREWORD

•

KAPPIYA CLASSICS

Hello Dear Readers

I am Tamizhiniya Tamizhdesan

when I was studying in school my teachers used to conduct lessons between many good books and that conduct gave me confidence that I can conduct more than a hundred topics with introductory speech. My Technical education helped a lot in this aspect. When I became a teacher I assisted my students in the way our teachers guided us.

My school, college and workplace friends lives scattered in different countries, the families of them too scattered in different nation, whereas I live in the Land of my Mother Language(Tamilnadu). Among my friends who are running to strive for their living, I have selected the publishing department to read their lives and pass it on to others. We are publishing legendary works under Kappiya Vasipagam. So far we have published more than 1500 books in package type.

I have used the library a lot in my school, college and work life. Novelist Vasu Murugavel writes that he brought a bundle of books from a person, read them and returned them. Similarly, I have imported hundreds of books read them and sent them back. I have also written novel in Tamil and English, also a book based on the Culture of Tamil People.

My son Imayakappiyan (8) started learning his Tamil lettering from the texts of our cover pages. The same way he is gaining the knowledge of book names, authors also the technical knowledge in publishing and helps us in many ways. My husband Tamizhdesan guides me about the packaging materials of the book contents and his creative thinking of book cover page makes me to create some unique cover pages. We three feel very happy to be in this field which makes us to learn continuously.

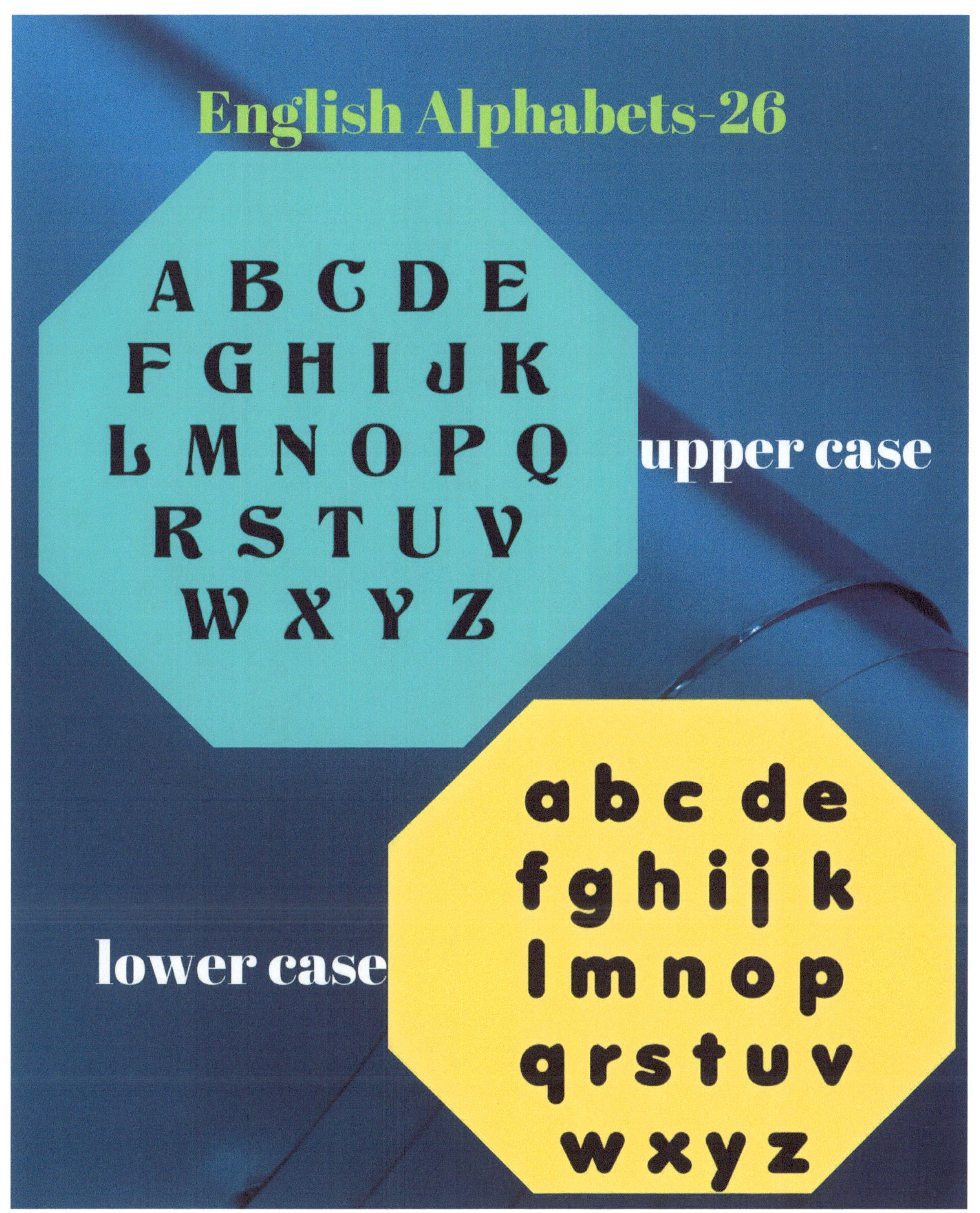
English Alphabets-26
A B C D E
F G H I J K
L M N O P Q
R S T U V
W X Y Z
upper case
lower case
a b c d e
f g h i j k
l m n o p
q r s t u v
w x y z

English cursive writing

I

A- Anhinga

Anhinga (Anhinga Anhinga)

Anhingas are a large yet slender-bodied waterbird species that primarily inhabit the warmer regions of the Americas.

These birds display a significant sexual dimorphism, with the males having an overall dark plumage and white bars on their wings. On the other hand, the females possess a tanned head and underparts, with yellow feet and legs. Anhingas have a widespread population throughout America and have many popular names, such as "Water Turkey," "Darter," and "Snakebird."
Wetland fish, both small and large, make up a majority of these birds' diets. Although, they're also known to feed on crustaceans and other invertebrates occasionally.

ANHINGA

II

B- Brandt's Cormorant

Brandt's Cormorant (Urile Penicillatus)

Named after Johann Friedrich von Brandt, a German naturalist, Brandt's Cormorants are large marine birds that have dark, glossy bodies. In the breeding season, these birds develop a bright blue throat patch.

Brandt's Cormorants are migratory birds that breed on the Pacific coast of North America. Rockfish and Herrings make up over 90% of their diet, although you might spot them going after shrimps and crabs once in a while.

BRANDT'S CORMORANT

III

C- Common Crane

Common Crane (Grus Grus)

Popularly known as the "Eurasian Crane" due to their widespread distribution throughout northern regions of Europe, the Common Cranes are medium-sized members of the crane family.

These cranes have a dark, slaty-grey body with a darker head and throat. Their upper tail coverts are shaped like explosive plumes, which are commonly used as a significant field identification mark by the birders.

COMMON CRANE

IV
D- Dunnock

Dunnock (Prunella Modularis)

Being the most widespread members of the accentor family, the Dunnocks are tiny passerine birds commonly found in the temperate areas of Europe and Asian Russia. These birds are also spotted in New Zealand, where they're an introduced species. Dunnocks are popular by several other names, such as "Hedge Sparrow," "Hedge Warbler," or "Hedge Accentor."

They're similar to a robin in size and have a brown body with paler underparts, except for their grey head. The adults are sexually monomorphic, with both sexes appearing identical.

DUNNOCK

V
E- Emu

Emu (Dromaius Novaehollandiae)

Declared as the second-largest bird species in the entire world, the Emus are a large, flightless bird species. They're endemic to Australia; while Australia was once home to other ratites, Emus are the only extant ratite species there today.

Emus are similar to the Ostriches; only they're smaller, shorter, and lighter in body mass than the latter. They have a small head, a long neck, and a wide body supported by two long legs. While these birds are flightless, they do have an incredible speed on the ground and can even run at a speed of over 31 miles per hour. Although both sexes of the adults have identical plumage, they do have other differences. The females are known to have a wider rump than their male counterparts and are also larger than them.

Emus have an average lifespan of 10-20 years in the wild and can survive up to 35 years in captivity.

EMU

VI

F- Fish Crow

Fish Crow (Corvus Ossifragus)

As their name suggests, the Fish Crows are a piscivore corvid species found in the eastern and southeastern parts of the United States. Although these corvids are closely related to the Tamaulipas and Sinaloa Crows, they resemble the American Crows in appearance. These birds are so similar superficially that it gets difficult to distinguish between them within their overlapping range.

However, the Fish Crows are smaller in size than them and have a glossier plumage. Both adult sexes have similar plumage and are sexually monomorphic. These birds have a distinctive, nasal call that sounds like "ark-ark-ark."

FISH CROW

VII
G- Gadwall

Gadwall (Mareca Strepera)

Found in northern Europe and central North America, the Gadwalls are the dabbling duck family members. These waterfowls are migratory in nature and travel south to Central America in the winter months.
The primary habitats of Gadwalls consist of marshes, open wetlands, and steppe lakes, with plenty of vegetation nearby. They primarily feed on plant matter but will also dive to catch aquatic prey when they get a chance.

Like most duck species, the Gadwalls are also strongly sexually dimorphic. The males have mainly grey plumage, with a black rump and touches of chestnut on their wings.
On the contrary, their female counterparts are mostly brown in color. The males are both larger and heavier than their female counterparts.

GADWALL

VIII
H- Hawaiian Hawk

Hawaiian Hawk (Buteo Solitarius)

As their name suggests, the Hawaiian Hawks are one of the two raptor species native to Hawaii, with the other one being Hawaiian Short-eared Owls.
The IUCN lists these hawks as Near Threatened Species; their population is under the threat of vehicle collisions and illegal shootings.
Hawaiian Hawks occur in two morphs, a dark one consisting of dark brown and a light one of grey. Out of these, the light morphs are more popular. They have a dark grey head and upper parts, with white undersides and dark spotting on the chest.
Both sexes of the adult Hawaiian Hawks harbor identical plumage; only the females are heavier than their male counterparts.

HAWAIIAN HAWK

IX
I- Ibisbill

Ibisbill (Ibidorhyncha Struthersii)

Ibisbills are a wader bird species commonly found across the Central Asian Plateau and the Himalayas. They are typically solitary birds, though sometimes spotted in little groups or flocks of eight birds.
Ibisbills are medium-sized and can be identified by their whitish belly, wretched crimson-colored bill, black face, and breast band.
Though both the counterparts are almost alike in appearance, the females have a longer bill than their male counterparts.

IBISBILL

X

J- Jacky Winter

Jacky Winter (Microeca Fascinans)

Named after their unique vocalizations, the Jacky Winters are small robin species found in Australia and Papua New Guinea. These birds commonly inhabit farmlands and open woodlands.

Jacky Winters have a dark grey head and plumage, with pale white underparts. On their wings and tail, you can notice a prominent white edge.

These robins are primarily insectivores and feed mostly on flying insects. Their call is rapid and strong, sounding something like "jacky-jacky-winter-winter."

JACKY WINTER

XI
K- Kagu

Kagu (Rhynochetos Jubatus)

Also spelled "Cage," the Kagus are a long-legged species belonging to the ground-dwelling bird family, Rhynchetidae. They're an endangered species that have a severe threat due to their increased predation.
Kagus have a striking white plumage with touches of ash-grey on their wings. This is highly unusual for a ground-dwelling bird and could be a probable reason behind their easy predation.
Kagus are nearly flightless and display minimal dimorphism between the adult sexes.

KAGU

L- Laughing Gull

Laughing Gull (Leucophaeus Atricilla)

Named after their laugh-like calls, the Laughing Gulls are a migratory gull species that have a widespread population in North and South America. These gulls have two subspecies.

Laughing Gulls are sexually monomorphic, but can you witness some changes in their plumage according to the season. In their breeding season, these wading birds have a dark hood on their face, dark wings, and tail, while the rest of their body is white.

They have a long, red bill and dark legs. During winters, their black hood grows considerably lighter in the shade.

LAUGHING GULL

XIII

M- Magpie Goose

Magpie Goose
(Anseranas Semipalmata)

Being the only living species of the Anseranatidae bird family, the Magpie Geese are medium-sized duck species. These waterfowls are commonly found in northern Australia and southern New Guinea.
Magpie Geese have the distinguishing feature of black and white plumage with yellowish legs. Although both the sexes of this species have a similar appearance, the males are larger than the females. They have a loud, honking call, which is often used as a field identification mark by the birders.
Magpie Geese mainly feed on the vegetable matter both on land and in water.

MAGPIE GOOSE

XIV

N- Noisy Pitta

Noisy Pitta (Pitta Versicolor)

The Noisy Pittas are an Australian Pitta species that inhabit the temperate, lowland, and montane forests of eastern Australia as well as New Guinea.

These birds might be small, but they're quite brightly colored, which makes them remarkable to the birders. They have a black head, with a dark chestnut crown and contrasting lemon yellow chest and belly.

On their lower belly, you can see another oval-shaped chestnut patch. Their back, including the wings, is covered in bright green, with turquoise edges to their wings.

Noisy Pittas are primarily insectivorous, feeding particularly on snails and earthworms.

NOISY PITTA

XV
O- Oilbird

Oilbird (Steatornis Caripensis)

Also referred to as the "Guácharo," the Oilbirds are the monotypic members of their genus, family, and order. They are primarily frugivores that have a nocturnal schedule, making them the only nocturnal, flying, fruit-eating bird species.

Oilbirds are common in South America and the Trinidad of the Caribbean. They're colonial birds that are closely related to the nightjars and nest in caves.

Oilbirds have a large but slim body, with a strongly hooked bill and small feet. They have a mainly reddish-brown plumage with white markings on their wings. Their underbody is colored in buff cinnamon and contains diamond-shaped markings all over.

These birds also have a remarkable, fan-shaped tail with stiff brown feathers. Due to their secretive personality, little is known about their sexual dimorphism.

OILBIRD

XVI

P- Pyrrhuloxia

Pyrrhuloxia (Cardinalis sinuatus)

Pyrrhuloxias are North American passerine songbirds commonly found across southwest America and northern Mexico. Usually inhabiting desert scrubs, mesquite thickets, and woodland areas, these birds are also commonly referred to as the "Desert Cardinals." Pyrrhuloxias have a brownish-grey body with red breasts and a mask. Their parrot-like, rounded bills are stout and yellow. These birds display sexual dimorphism in their plumage, with males having more red in their plumes than their female counterparts.
Fruits, seeds, and insects make up the primary diet of the Desert Cardinals.

PYRRHULOXIA

XVII

Q- Queen Whydah

Queen Whydah (Vidua Regia)

Queen Whydahs are African passerine birds that are sized similar to the sparrows. These birds have a quite widespread distribution within Africa and are declared to be a Least Concern species by the IUCN.
These birds can commonly be found in the grasslands and other open habitats in the southern parts of Africa. They're primarily seed-eaters, with different varieties of seeds and grains making up over 90% of their diet.
The adult Queen Wydahs display sexual dimorphism in their breeding plumage. The breeding males have a jet-black crown atop their head, dark upperparts, and elongated tail shaft feathers, which lends them their other name, the "Shaft-tailed Whydah." Their underbody is bright yellow in contrast.
Outside of the breeding season, both sexes display a dull, olive-brown plumage which makes it easier for them to blend into their surroundings and avoid predation.

QUEEN WHYDAH

XVIII
R- Roseate Spoonbill

Roseate Spoonbill (Platalea Ajaja)

The Roseate Spoonbills are large, non-migratory spoonbill species found in North and South America. These birds lack sexual dimorphism, with both sexes having a pale greenish head, a pinkish plumage, and elongated neck, legs, and bill.
The color of their plumage is derived from their carotene-rich diet and can, thus, vary in different seasons.

ROSEATE SPOONBILL

Enter Caption

XIX
S- Sooty Grouse

Sooty Grouse
(Dendragapus Fuliginosus)

Sooty Grouses are a forest grouse species native to the Pacific Coast of North America. These birds naturally inhabit coniferous and mixed forests across mountainous regions. Though permanent residents, they might move to denser forests in the winter months.

Sooty Grouses are medium-sized grouses having a long tail with a slight grey tone at the tip. The adults display significant sexual dimorphism in plumage. The males usually have a dark appearance with a yellow throat air sac that is enclosed by white. They also feature a yellow wattle over the eye.

On the other hand, their female counterparts are between mottled brown to dark brown, having white patches on their underparts. Sooty Grouses thrive on green plants, berries, and insects.

SOOTY GROUSE

XX

T- Toco Toucan

Toco Toucan (Ramphastos Toco)

Also known as "Giant Toucan," the Toco Toucans are the largest member of the toucan family. These toucans are native to South America and are a popular attraction at zoos.

Toco Toucans have two recognized subspecies and mainly black plumage, much like that of all other toucans. Only their face and throat are colored in a white patch, with a large, orange bill, with a reddish base and a dark spot on the tip.

The irises of these toucans are bluish, with orangish shade surrounding them. The adult males are larger in size than their female counterparts, but all that's all the external difference you can see between the sexes.

TOCO TOUCAN

XXI

U- Usambara Eagle-Owl

Usambara Eagle-Owl
(Bubo Vosseleri)

Also referred to as the "Vosseier's Eagle-owl," the Usambara Eagle-owls are a large true owl species endemic to Africa. They're found in abundance in the Usambara Mountains in Tanzania, after which they've been named.

Although Usambara Eagle-owls initially started as an individual species, they're now placed as a subspecies of the Fraser's Eagle-owls. They're among the larger members of the owl family, with a tawny brown head and upper body covered in heavy bars.

Their facial disc is pale tawny in color, with buff undersides covered in brown blotches and black bars. Their legs and feet are whitish, with dull yellowish irises and a bluish-white bill.

USAMBARA EAGLE-OWL

XXII
V- Verdin

Verdin (Auriparus Flaviceps)

Verdins are a tiny penduline tit species endemic to North America. These birds inhabit shrubs and thorny thickets with few trees.

Verdins have a greyish appearance, pale plumage, and their head is bright yellow. Their rufus shoulder patches and sharply pointed bills are the other characteristics of these birds.

Verdins are insectivorous and prefer catching their prey among the scrubs and desert trees. They also eat fruits, berries, and often nectars obtained from hummingbird feeders.

VERDIN

XXIII

W- Wild Turkey

Wild Turkey
(Meleagris Gallopavo)

Wild Turkeys are large poultry birds that are endemic to North America. They inhabit hardwood and mixed-conifer hardwood forests with dispersed openings like fields, orchards, and pastures.

Wild Turkeys have long legs that are reddish-yellow or greyish-green. These birds display strong sexual dimorphism.

The males are called "gobblers" and have a large, featherless red head, a reddish throat, and red wattles on their neck and throat. Their long, fan-shaped tail is dark, and their wings have a shiny bronze look. Males also characterize a thick beard growing from the center of their breast.

The female Wild Turkeys are called "hens" and have low-key feathers marked with brown and grey. Their beard is thinner than their male counterparts. Males are larger than their female counterparts.

WILD TURKEY

XXIV
X- Xantus's Hummingbird

Xantus's Hummingbird
(Basilinna Xantusii)

The Xantus's Hummingbirds are a tiny North American hummingbird species that have been named after John Xantus de Vesey, the Hungarian zoologist. These birds have a widespread population within their range and can be found in a variety of habitats, including urban and suburban areas.

The adult Xantus's Hummingbirds have a mainly dark green plumage, with their head and upper parts being darker than the undersides. They have two white eye stripes that stand in strong contrast with their otherwise dark face.

Their bill is orangish in color, with a black tip and cinnamon brown underbody. The males have a glossy green throat, which is absent in their female counterparts.

Like all hummingbirds, Xantus's Hummingbirds also feed on nectar primarily but will also catch flying insects occasionally.

XANTUS'S HUMMINGBIRD

XXV
Y- Yellow-Eared Parrot

Yellow-Eared Parrot
(Ognorhynchus Icterotis)

The Yellow-eared Parrots are a South American parrot species found in the mountains of Andes, Colombia. The large-scale clearing of montane forests within their habitat range has led to a steep decline in their population, making them a Vulnerable species.
These primarily fruit-eating parrots have a large body and a long tail, colored mainly in green. Their head and upper body are bright leaf-green, while the underparts are paler, somewhat lime green in appearance.
On the face of these parrots, you can see patches of yellow, particularly around their eyes and ears, which lends them their name.
Yellow-eared Parrots possess a dark, hooked bill, with the adults displaying sexual monomorphism.

YELLOW-EARED PARROT

XXVI

Z- Zanzibar Red Bishop

Zanzibar Red Bishop
(Euplectes Nigroventis)

Named after the island they're endemic to, Zanzibar Red Bishops are a weaver species found in East Africa. These birds primarily inhabit moist areas, marshes, flooded grasslands, and cultivated areas; their range often overlaps with the Black-winged Bishops.

The adult Zanzibar Red Bishops are sexually dimorphic, with the breeding males appearing different from the non-breeding males and females.

The breeding males are colored in bright orange and black. While their head and upper parts are orange, the underbody is black in contrast, except for a bold orange breast band.

On the other hand, the non-breeding males and females have a dull brown, streaky plumage. They lack both the breast band and the luster of the breeding males.

Zanzibar Red Bishops have a short, typically rough call that sounds like "tek tek tek."

ZANZIBAR
RED BISHOP